THE PLAYLET SERIES

# KEY CHAIN

An English play in 15 scenes about KEYS

For Years 6, 7 and 8 (Level 3/1)


By John Middleton

Bibliografische Information der Deutschen
Nationalbibliothek:
Die Deutsche Nationalbibliothek verzeichnet diese
Publikation in der Deutschen Nationalbibliografie;
detaillierte bibliografische Daten sind im Internet über
http://dnb.dnb.de abrufbar.

United States Copyright Office

1-8168934481

Herstellung und Verlag: BoD – Books on Demand,
Norderstedt

ISBN: 978-3-7504-3336-6

Other plays from THE PLAYLET SERIES by John Middleton:

LUCKY CHARMS – a play in 10 scenes about LUCK for
Years 6, 7 and 8 (Level 3/2)

STAND UP – a play in 8 scenes about MORAL COURAGE
for Years 8, 9 and 10 (Level 4/1)

# CONTENTS

## FOREWARD

KEY CHAIN is a play for students in Years 6, 7 or 8 (Level 3/1). It is designed for a normal-sized English class and for students with varying interests in acting. Since there are 49 roles – none of which are really minor – students who enjoy acting can perform in several scenes and play to their heart's content, whereas students who aren't particularly keen on acting only have one role to master in one single scene. Every scene deals with a key, big keys and small keys, new keys and old keys, keys that lock doors and keys that open hearts, keys that are lost and keys that are found, keys that bring people together and keys that bring people apart. There are monologues, dialogues and scenes with as many as eight or nine performers. The themes are geared to the experiences of students today – such as friendship, bullying, infatuation and rejection – and offer young actresses and actors the opportunity to discover a wide variety of feelings while performing. The plots are believable and understandable, the language is idiomatic and easily accessible for English learners. KEY CHAIN works well when performed for smaller audiences: parents and other classes. But it can also be highly entertaining for a large audience. Performing time: about one hour. Of course, it is also possible to select individual scenes and perform them as simple skits outside the context of the KEY CHAIN. In that case it is still recommendable to create a suitable setting for presenting the skits to an audience. The true joy of performing a foreign-language play is to feel it click, to realize that the people watching the performance don't only "get the picture", they are also delighted to see a story come to life when presented in English by non-native performers.

– John Middleton, Hamburg, 2019

## PROLOGUE

*(Two MCs come out on stage, two girls.)*

MC1

Ladies and gentlemen, boys and girls, key lovers and key haters.

MC2

We are going to present fifteen scenes about keys.

MC1

Big keys and small keys.

MC2

New keys and old keys.

MC1

Keys that lock doors and keys that open hearts.

MC2

Keys that are lost and keys that are found.

MC1

Keys that bring people together and keys that bring people apart.

MC2

Hey, you know what I hate about the key to my house?

MC1

No, what?

MC2

I always lose it.

MC1

It's important to have a second key.

MC2

Sure, but I always lose the second key, too.

MC1

Then you need a key with a built-in beeper that beeps whenever you are looking for it.

MC2

What do you mean?

MC1

If I lose my key, I pull out the beeper control and push it. And my key starts to beep. Like this…

*(We hear a beep.)*

MC2

But what if I lose the beeper control?

MC1

Then you need a beeper control for the beeper control.

MC2

And what if I lose the beeper control for the beeper control?

MC1

Then you need a beeper control for the beeper control for the beeper control.

MC2

And what if I lose the beeper control for the beeper control for the beeper control?

MC1

Then don't lock your door.

MC2

That's a good idea. Thanks.

## SCENE 1        THE LOCKED BIKE

*(A boy, Jimmy, is standing in front of his bike. It is locked. He tries to open the lock, but something is wrong. He shakes the lock and is very angry.)*

JIMMY

I don't believe it! This is the second time this week that I lost the key to my bike lock. My parents are going to kill me!

*(A girl comes by, Jennifer, and watches as Jimmy tries everything to unlock his bike. Jimmy notices Jennifer. He is still very angry.)*

JIMMY

What do you want?

JENNIFER

I was just watching you.

JIMMY

Why?

JENNIFER

Because you have a problem, and maybe I can help you.

JIMMY

Oh yeah? What problem do you think I have?

JENNIFER

You lost the key to your bike lock.

JIMMY

How do you know that?

JENNIFER

I know lots of things about you, Jimmy Blue.

JIMMY

What did you call me?

JENNIFER

Jimmy Blue. You know, like the Blues. You always look so sad, like you have the Blues.

JIMMY

What are you trying to tell me?

JENNIFER

That maybe I can help you.

JIMMY

I don't need any of your help. So, just leave me alone and get lost.

JENNIFER

What's your real problem, Jimmy Blue? It isn't just your lost key, is it?

JIMMY

I have to go to my guitar lessons.

JENNIFER

And you need your bike to get there?

JIMMY

Right.

JENNIFER

And what if you don't go?

JIMMY

If I don't go, my parents will kill me, because they pay lots of money for my guitar lessons.

JENNIFER

Do you like to play the guitar?

JIMMY

Sure, but I hate the lessons.

JENNIFER

Did you tell your parents?

JIMMY

Yes, but they want me to be a famous rock star like Jimmy Hendrix.

JENNIFER

That's cool. Jimmy Hendrix was great.

JIMMY

Yeah, sure. But my guitar teacher is a real idiot.

JENNIFER

I know.

JIMMY

What? How do you know about my guitar teacher?

JENNIFER

He's my brother.

JIMMY

I don't believe it. What's your name?

JENNIFER

Jennifer. Jennifer Biggs.

JIMMY

And Tommy Biggs is your brother?

JENNIFER

Yeah. He isn't only a terrible guitar teacher. He's also a terrible brother.

JIMMY

I'm sorry I said that about your brother.

JENNIFER

Don't be sorry. You know, I also give guitar lessons. Here's my number if you ever want a new guitar teacher.

*(Jennifer hands Jimmy a card.)*

JIMMY

Thanks.

JENNIFER

By the way, is this yours?

*(Jennifer hands Jimmy a key.)*

JIMMY

Hey, it's my key. Where did you find it?

JENNIFER

It was on the floor in front of your locker.

JIMMY

Thanks.

JENNIFER

Take care, Jimmy Blue.

*(Jimmy looks at the card and reads the number.)*

JIMMY

"172345677. Jennifer Biggs, guitar lessons for young rock stars." Cool.

## SCENE 2     OCCUPIED

*(A boy is standing outside a restroom. The door is apparently locked. He knocks.)*

JESSE

Tony?

TONY *(off stage)*

Jesse?

JESSE

That you?

TONY *(off stage)*

Yeah.

JESSE

Hurry!

TONY *(off stage)*

Can't.

JESSE

Why not?

TONY *(off stage)*

Big job.

JESSE

Number 1?

TONY *(off stage)*

Number 2.

JESSE

I'm dying!

TONY *(off stage)*

Number 1?

JESSE

Number 2.

TONY *(off stage)*

Go outside!

JESSE

No way!

TONY *(off stage)*

Okay.

JESSE

Okay what?

TONY *(off stage)*

Almost finished.

JESSE

Idiot!

TONY *(off stage)*

Keep cool.

JESSE

Faster!

TONY *(off stage)*

Magic word?

JESSE

Please.

TONY *(off stage)*

Nice.

*(We hear a toilet flushing.)*

JESSE

Finished?

TONY *(off stage)*

Yeah.

JESSE

Open up!

TONY *(off stage)*

Just a sec.

JESSE

Can't wait!

TONY *(off stage)*

Oh no!

JESSE

What?

TONY *(off stage)*
Won't open.
JESSE
What?
TONY *(off stage)*
The door.
JESSE
No way!
TONY *(off stage)*
The key!
JESSE
What key?
TONY *(off stage)*
Broken.
JESSE
No way!
*(We hear Tony laughing.)*
JESSE
What's up?
*(The door opens. Tony comes outside, holding the key.)*
TONY
Just joking.
JESSE
Idiot!
TONY
Keep cool!
*(Jesse enters the toilet and shuts the door.)*
JESSE *(off stage)*
Oh no!
TONY
Problem?
JESSE *(off stage)*
Key?

TONY
Here.
*(Tony locks the door from the outside.)*
JESSE  *(off stage)*
Don't!
TONY
Idiot!
JESSE  *(off stage)*
No way!
TONY
Problem?
JESSE  *(off stage)*
Toilet paper!
TONY
Sorry!
JESSE  *(off stage)*
Help!
*(Tony walks away laughing.)*

## SCENE 3          COLLAPSE

*(A boy, Gary, walks across the stage past a girl, Sue.)*

GARY

Hi.

*(Sue doesn't answer. The boy suddenly collapses in pain. He moans and groans and rolls all over the floor. The girl comes running over to him and bends down. She helps him get up.)*

SUE

What's wrong? Can I help you?

GARY

I don't know what's happening.

SUE

Here, sit down on this chair.

*(She helps him sit down.)*

GARY

I'm sorry to bother you.

SUE

It's no bother. Tell me where it hurts.

GARY

Up here.

*(He points to his heart.)*

SUE

Your heart?

GARY

Yes.

SUE

What does it feel like?

GARY

It feels better now.

*(She touches his heart.)*

SUE

Does this hurt?

GARY

No, that makes it feel better.

SUE

Do you have a temperature?

*(She feels his forehead.)*

SUE

Your forehead seems cool. I don't think you have a temperature.

GARY

No, I'm feeling much better now.

SUE

What did it feel like when you collapsed?

GARY

It felt like my heart just closed up, as if it was locked.

SUE

You felt like your heart was locked?

GARY

Yeah, it was all tight and closed up.

SUE

Do you have heart problems?

*(She feels his pulse.)*

GARY

No.

SUE

Heart problems in the family?

GARY

No.

SUE

But you feel better now?

GARY

Much better.

SUE

And your heart?

GARY

It feels like it's opening up.

SUE

What do you mean?

GARY

It feels like you unlocked it.

SUE

Like I did what?

GARY

My heart was locked, and you came and opened it.

SUE

Is this a joke?

GARY

No, I'm serious. You have the key to my heart.

SUE

I have the key to your heart? What do you mean?

GARY

I see you every day and think: What a great girl. I wish I knew her. And then I say hi to you, but you never even notice.

SUE

I'm sorry, but I don't think I ever saw you before.

GARY

And I see you every day. Thank you.

SUE

For what?

GARY

For opening my heart.

*(Gary gives her something.)*

SUE

What's this.

*(It's a key.)*

GARY

It's the key to my heart, so you can open it when you see me tomorrow.

SUE

What should I do?

GARY

Just say hi when I say hi to you.

SUE

And that will open your heart?

GARY

Yes.

SUE

What's your name?

GARY

Gary Jensen.

SUE

See you tomorrow, Gary Jensen.

GARY

See you tomorrow, Sue.

## SCENE 4        DETENTION

*(A girl, Mary Ann, and a boy, Paul, are sitting at a desk.)*

MARY ANN

How much longer?

PAUL

That's the tenth time you asked me.

MARY ANN

So what? Just answer the question.

PAUL

I answered it a minute ago.

MARY ANN

How much longer, wise guy?

PAUL

A minute ago it was 15 minutes.

MARY ANN

And now?

PAUL

15 minus 1 is 14.

MARY ANN

14 what?

PAUL

14 minutes! We have 14 minutes left in detention.

MARY ANN

I can't stand it here! I have to get out!

PAUL

I really don't think it's so bad.

MARY ANN

What? It's the worst thing in the world!

PAUL

It gives me a chance to be together with you.

MARY ANN

What?

PAUL

It's the only reason I'm in detention. I got in trouble, so I could be in detention with you.

MARY ANN

You're crazy!

PAUL

I've wanted to talk to you for so long.

MARY ANN

I'm leaving.

PAUL

Don't. You'll get in trouble, Mary Ann.

MARY ANN

So what?

PAUL

And you'll get detention for a whole week.

MARY ANN

I don't care.

PAUL

Sit down, Mary Ann.

*(She gets up and goes to the door. It's locked.)*

MARY ANN

I don't believe it.

PAUL

What?

MARY ANN

It's locked!

PAUL

Of course, it's locked.

MARY ANN

They can't just lock the door.

PAUL

Sure, they can.

MARY ANN

What if there was a fire in here? How would we get out? We'd burn to death.

PAUL

No, we wouldn't. They'd unlock the door for us.

MARY ANN

They can't do this to me!

*(She becomes hysterical.)*

MARY ANN

I feel dizzy. I feel sick. Everything is turning around and around. Help me! I can't breathe! I have to get out of here!

PAUL

Calm down. Everything's okay.

*(He tries to touch her and comfort her.)*

MARY ANN

Don't touch me! Don't ever touch me again! I'm going crazy!

PAUL

Hey, everything's okay. Everything's fine.

MARY ANN

Get me out of here, or I'll start a fire!

*(Paul unlocks the door.)*

MARY ANN *(completely normal again)*

What? You had a key the whole time? I don't believe it. And you didn't open the door? What an idiot!

PAUL

I'm sorry. I just wanted to…

MARY ANN

Don't ever talk to me again.

*(Mary Ann hurries out of the room.)*

## SCENE 5        ANGELS

*(A girl, Sarah, appears on stage with a little box in her hands.)*
SARAH

I never knew him. He died when I was only two. And this is all I have left. It isn't really mine. It actually belongs to my mother. And she belongs to my stepfather who I hate. So, I really feel it's mine. Like I said, it's all I have left of my father. Lots of little things he left behind. Pictures and souvenirs and stuff like that, like the first baby teeth he lost. My mother showed me everything once, but that was a long time ago. And every time I asked if I could take another look at what's inside she told me that she'd lost the key. I mean, how could she lose the key to the lockbox with all this important stuff that belonged to the love of her life? He was the only man she ever really loved. That's what she told me. I can't really remember what's in it? I bet there's something in it that he really wanted me to have. My mother said he really loved me before he was killed in that car accident. He called me his little angel. He said I looked like an angel. He said I was the best thing that ever happened to him. He said, with me in his life it was like heaven on earth. And now he's in the other heaven, the one up there.

*(She points upward.)*
SARAH

I wonder if I could break it open?

*(She drops the box and it is suddenly open. She picks it up.)*
SARAH

It's open. What should I do? Should I look inside? What will I find? What if the box is empty? What if there's nothing important in it? What if he didn't real care about me? What if I wasn't really his angel. Should I open it or not?

*(She opens the box and smiles. Then she pulls something out.)*
SARAH

An angel… And another angel and another one and another one. The box is full of angels.

*(She is holding a "paper doll chain" that looks like angels holding hands. She looks up.)*
SARAH
Thank you, Daddy.

## SCENE 6        GHOST

*(Nine boys – Ken, Phil, Billy, John, Tom, Paul, Terry, Ron and Sam – are in a cellar. They have been drinking Coke and juice, but they pretend that it's alcohol. They act like they are drunk. They are laughing and being silly and telling stupid jokes.)*

TOM

Why is six afraid of seven?

PAUL

I don't know.

TOM

Because six heard that seven ATE nine. Understand? Eat – ate. Seven ATE nine.

*(The boys laugh.)*

KEN

What a stupid joke.

TERRY

I got a joke. Why did the boy take a ladder to school?

PHIL

Because he wanted to get high.

TERRY

Not bad. But the real answer is: Because he wanted to go to high school.

*(The boys laugh.)*

SAM

Hey Billy, do you have any jokes?

BILLY

Yeah. Did you ever see the film KING KONG? The way King Kong climbed up the Empire State Building?

PHIL

Yeah, it was okay. But I thought it was really stupid how King Kong fell in love with that woman.

BILLY

I got a joke about King Kong. What's really big and hairy and climbs the Empire State Building wearing a dress?

JOHN

No idea.

TOM

I don't know.

BILLY

Queen Kong.

*(The boys laugh.)*

PAUL

What a stupid joke!

TERRY

I'll drink to that.

*(Terry raises his glass.)*

RON

Hey, give me some more of that whisky. My glass is empty.

SAM

Don't drink too much or you'll get sick. Remember what happened at Christmas?

KEN

Here, try some of this rum. It's really great.

RON

Thanks.

PHIL

What happened at Christmas?

BILLY

Didn't you hear about it?

SAM

Ron was at Susan's house for Christmas Dinner, and they gave him some champagne. And when they were having dinner, Ron got sick on the turkey.

EVERYBODY

Yuck!

JOHN *(to Ron)*

I don't believe it. You really got sick at the table?

TOM

And he threw up all over the turkey and the potatoes.

PAUL

Nobody could eat it, so they went to McDonald's for Christmas Dinner.

TERRY

And Ron went home to bed.

*(Everybody laughs.)*

RON

Okay, okay, but this is different.

SAM *(acting like he's drunk)*

Oh, I'm so drunk, I don't think I can even walk straight.

*(He gets up and wobbles around and falls on the floor.)*

RON

Hey, Sam. How much have you had to drink? You're totally drunk.

SAM *(gets up and acts quite drunk)*

I've had two bottles of whisky and ten beers.

TERRY *(gets up and acts drunk)*

Oh, that's nothing. I've had 20 beers and seven bottles of rum.

PAUL *(gets up and falls down)*

Oh, that's nothing. You guys are just beginners. I've had 15 bottles of wine and 50 bottles of beer.

JOHN *(gets up and wobbles around)*

That's nothing. I can drink lots more than you guys. I've had 100 bottles of beer and 200 bottles of vodka.

TOM

You guys are crazy. If you drank that much alcohol, you'd be dead.

SAM

How do you know? You've never had any alcohol in your whole life.

KEN

Yeah, you got no idea what alcohol tastes like!

PHIL

You're no fun, Tom. You never want to try anything new.

BILLY

You're a real party pooper!

EVERYBODY BUT TOM

Party pooper! Party pooper!

TOM

If that's how you guys feel, then I'm going home!

EVERYBODY BUT TOM

Party pooper! Party pooper!

TOM

And I'm going to tell my parents that you're all drunk!

*(Tom leaves.)*

EVERYBODY BUT TOM

Party pooper! Party pooper!

PAUL

I'm so drunk I'm going to get sick.

*(He pretends to throw up.)*

JOHN

I'm going to get sick, too.

*(He pretends to throw up, too.)*

TERRY

Watch out! I'm going to throw up!

SAM

Oh no! Me, too!

*(Terry and Sam also pretend to throw up. Everybody laughs. Suddenly we hear Tom.)*

TOM

Hey, who locked the door?

KEN

What do you mean?

TOM

The cellar door is locked. And there's no key.

PHIL

Don't be stupid. The cellar door was open just five minutes ago when I went to the toilet.

BILLY

We never lock the cellar door, because we don't have a key. We lost it after my grandfather died.

*(We hear a noise, like coughing, from backstage.)*

JOHN

Hey, what was that?

TOM

It sounded like someone coughing.

BILLY

But who could it be? We're the only ones in the cellar.

*(We hear the noise again.)*

PAUL

None of us are missing, so it must be someone else.

TERRY

I'm going to take a look.

*(Terry walks backstage. Then he comes back in and looks very frightened.)*

RON

What's wrong? It looks like you saw a ghost.

TERRY

I did.

*(At that moment someone comes in wearing a bed sheet. It looks like a ghost. All the boys scream.)*

SAM

Hey, who are you?

JEANNIE *(Billy's sister, wearing a bed sheet)*

I'm the ghost of Billy's grandfather.

KEN

No way!

PHIL

Prove it!

JEANNIE

I died two years ago after drinking too much vodka.

BILLY

That's right. He's right. My grandfather killed himself with alcohol. He was an alcoholic and drank himself to death.

JEANNIE

And now, Billy, you are killing yourself with alcohol. You and your friends.

JOHN

Hey, we aren't drinking alcohol.

TOM

I want to go home.

BILLY

Grandpa, we were just having fun.

JEANNIE

Alcohol is no fun. Alcohol is a killer.

PAUL

We aren't drunk, sir!

JEANNIE

I am going to call your parents. They will be here in a minute. And I will tell them that you have been drinking.

RON

But we didn't do anything wrong.

SAM

Here, smell our drinks. It's just Coke and Fanta and juice.

JEANNIE

Alright, if you promise me you'll never drink any alcohol for the rest of your lives, I won't call your parents.

EVERYBODY

We promise. We promise.

TOM

Come on, let us out. I want to go home.

JEANNIE

Alright, I'll open the door.

*(At that moment Jeannie's bed sheet falls off, and everyone sees that it's Billy's sister.)*

BILLY

Jeannie! What are you doing here?

TERRY

You mean, that isn't your grandfather's ghost?

BILLY

No, it's my stupid sister.

EVERYBODY

No way!

BILLY

Jeannie, I'm going to kill you!

JEANNIE

You have to catch me first.

*(Jeannie runs away and Billy runs after her.)*

## Scene 7 BASKETBALL

*(A boy, Jackie, appears on stage with a basketball. He dribbles a bit, then he stops, walks closer to the audience and starts talking.)*

JACKIE

Hi, I'm Jackie Thomas. I shouldn't be here, you know? I'm not allowed to be in the gym. I'm not allowed to be here at school anymore, because they kicked me out.

*(He dribbles the ball again and takes a shot at an imaginary basket.)*

JACKIE

I was on the basketball team. I was really good. I mean, I am really good at basketball, but the coach never let me play. Just once, in the final minute… when we were losing by 20 points.

*(He walks over and picks up the ball again.)*

JACKIE

I always hoped Coach Williams would see how good I was and that I would be one of the starting five, you know, the five players who start and usually play most of the game. Every Friday morning before the big game on Friday evening Coach Williams hangs up the list of the starting five.

*(He dribbles again.)*

JACKIE

But my name was never on the list.

*(He takes another shot at the imaginary basket.)*

JACKIE

So one Thursday evening after practice I waited in the shower room until all the players had left. Then I hid in the locker room until Coach Williams was gone. I went into his office, and there on his desk was the list with the starting five that he was going to hang up the next morning. Like always, my name wasn't on it.

*(He walks over and picks up the basketball again.)*

JACKIE

So I sat down at Coach Williams' old typewriter. I knew how to use it, because my grandmother has an old typewriter, and she let me use it when I was little.

*(He dribbles the ball again.)*

JACKIE

I typed up a new starting five list, and my name was at the top of the list: JACKIE THOMAS, point guard. It felt so cool to see my name at the top of the starting five. I made ten copies and hung them up all over school, so everybody could see that I was a starter.

*(He shoots again at the imaginary basket. We hear the sound of a crowd cheering.)*

JACKIE

Before the first lesson all my classmates seemed really impressed. That beautiful girl Kathy came up to me and said, "Respect, Jackie. What are you doing after the game?"

*(He walks over and picks up the ball again.)*

JACKIE

During the second lesson there was a knock at the door. Coach Williams was standing outside with two big security guys.

*(He dribbles the ball.)*

JACKIE

They took me to the office where my parents were waiting for me. They made me hand in all my books, and they said I could never set foot on the school grounds again.

*(He shoots at the imaginary basket. The sound of cheers.)*

JACKIE

My parents sent me away to a private school that didn't have a basketball team, so now I practice on my own at the playground near the dormitory where I stay. And whenever I'm back home again, I come over to the old school gym and play basketball all night, because I still have the key I stole from Coach Williams.

*(He picks up the ball again.)*

JACKIE

And one day when I'm an NBA basketball player starring for the Dallas Mavericks I know that Coach Williams is going to feel really sorry he didn't put me on the starting five.

*(The sound of cheers.)*

## SCENE 8       BULLY

*(Joe is a bully, and he loves to bully Leonardo. Leonardo is walking across the stage. Joe is standing in the audience.)*

JOE

Hey, why the big rush? Where are you going in such a hurry? Are the cops chasing you?

LEONARDO

My mom is waiting for me in the car.

JOE

Oh, I see. Mommy is waiting for you. Isn't that nice? It must be so wonderful to have such a nice mommy like that who waits for you after school.

*(Joe walks on stage and stands in front of Leonardo.)*

LEONARDO

I have a doctor's appointment.

JOE

Oh, is little Leonardo ill? Does little Leonardo have an ouchie?

LEONARDO

It's because of my headaches.

JOE

Oh, little Leonardo has headaches, does he?

*(Joe pushes Leonardo who falls on the floor.)*

JOE

Oh, little Leonardo. What happened? Did you fall down and hurt yourself?

LEONARDO

I have to hurry, because…

JOE

I know, Mommy is waiting.

*(Leonardo tries to get up, but Joe pushes him down again.)*

LEONARDO

I have to hurry. It's very important.

JOE

Say the magic word.

LEONARDO

Please.

JOE

Say "please, Joe, I'll do whatever you want."

LEONARDO

Please, Joe. I'll do whatever you want.

JOE

Okay, tell me where the Biology teacher put my cell phone. He took it from me during the Biology lesson.

LEONARDO

They keep all the cell phones in that room.

*(Leonardo points to a door.)*

JOE

In there?

*(Joe looks at the door.)*

JOE

How do you know that?

LEONARDO

I'm a teacher's assistant, so I know lots of things like that.

JOE

That's cool. Okay, you go in there and get my cell phone, and I'll let you run outside to Mommy.

LEONARDO

How?

JOE

How what?

LEONARDO

How do I know which cell phone is yours? There are at least 50 cell phones in there.

JOE

Okay, listen. I'll go in there and get my phone, and you stay out here and make sure that no teachers come.

LEONARDO

Okay.

*(Leonardo unlocks the door. Joe enters. Leonardo shuts the door and locks it.)*

JOE

Hey, where's the light switch?

LEONARDO

It's on the right, next to the door.

JOE

Ah, there it is… Hey, it doesn't work.

LEONARDO

Maybe it's broken.

JOE

I'll just open the door a bit, so I can see where my phone is.

*(We hear Joe trying to open the door from the other side.)*

JOE

Hey, what's going on? The door is locked.

LEONARDO

Oh no, how terrible for you.

*(Leonardo laughs.)*

JOE

Open the door right now, or I'll…

LEONARDO

What will you do?

JOE

I'll kill you.

LEONARDO

Big words from somebody who's in big trouble.

JOE

What do you mean?

**LEONARDO**

That's the room where they keep the school safe with thousands of dollars. When they find you in there, they'll arrest you for robbery.

**JOE**

You can't do this to me. If I get in trouble once more, they'll kick me out of school.

**LEONARDO**

How sad. I will really miss you. You know, you're one of my best friends. Really.

**JOE**

Let me out!

**LEONARDO**

What's the magic word?

**JOE**

Please.

**LEONARDO**

No.

**JOE**

Please, I'll do whatever you want.

**LEONARDO**

No.

**JOE**

Please, I'll give you my cell phone and my iPad.

**LEONARDO**

No, that isn't the magic word either.

**JOE**

But my parents will kill me if I get kicked out of school. They'll send me to a military academy.

**LEONARDO**

Tough luck. Oh well, I'm sorry I have to leave. My mom is waiting for me.

JOE

Don't leave me here.

LEONARDO

I'll just call up the security guys. I'm sure they'll let you out.

*(Leonardo acts like he's calling somebody.)*

LEONARDO

Hello, Security? This is Leonardo Jenkins. I saw a student, Joe McDonald, go into Room 24 where you keep the safe… Yes, I locked the door… That's fine. Goodbye.

*(Leonardo quietly unlocks the door and walks away.)*

JOE

Don't leave me alone! Leonardo, please! I'll never bully you again. Please, Leonardo. I'll do anything you want… Leonardo? Leonardo?

*(We see the door slowly open.)*

JOE

Hey, the door isn't locked anymore.

*(Joe comes out and looks around.)*

JOE *(hesitantly)*

No security?

*(now loud and threatening)*

Okay, Leonardo, the next time I see you, I'll kill you.

## SCENE )        MOTHERS AND DAUGHTERS

*(Two mothers are sitting at a café: Ms. Liz Phelps and Ms. Sue Taylor.)*

LIZ

I wish I had a son and not such a terrible daughter.

SUE

I know what you mean. My daughter is such a problem, too.

LIZ

Christine's room is always a mess. She throws her clothes all over the place, and when I try to tidy up and wash her dirty clothes, she screams and throws me out of the room.

SUE

Can't you clean up her room when she's at school?

LIZ

No, because she locks her door.

SUE

Don't you have an extra key?

LIZ

She changed the lock, and I don't have a key.

SUE

My daughter's room is a mess, too, but I won't clean it for her.

LIZ

Does she lock her door?

SUE

No, I lock it, so no one else has to see the mess.

LIZ

Does she leave her clothes everywhere, too?

SUE

No, Lina leaves food everywhere. Used plates and cups and leftover food.

LIZ

That's awful. Aren't you afraid of insects and rats?

SUE

Sure, but the last time I cleaned up Lina's room when she wasn't home, she protested by not eating anything for a whole week.

LIZ

Christine never eats anything but yoghurt, because she wants to be a model.

SUE

I'm so worried about Lina, because she eats so much. And she's getting fatter every day.

LIZ

How about social networking?

SUE

What do you mean?

LIZ

Does Lina spend a lot of time online with things like Instagram?

SUE

No, after she had a very bad experience chatting, she stopped using the computer. Now she spends hours writing in her diary.

LIZ

That's great.

SUE

I'm not so sure if it's really so great.

LIZ

Why not?

SUE

I have the feeling that she's always writing terrible things about me.

LIZ

Well, at least she keeps it in a diary that nobody else reads. Christine posts everything on Facebook. She writes about every argument we have and she's always taking pictures of me that she posts online. Like when I get out of bed in the morning – she takes my picture. It's terrible. People I don't even know come up to me at the supermarket and say I should be nicer to my daughter.

SUE

Do you remember what it was like with your mother?

LIZ

For one thing, we didn't have the Internet.

SUE

Yeah, but didn't you argue with your mother?

LIZ

Sure, I tried to, but then she grounded me.

SUE

For how long?

LIZ

Usually for two weeks. I could only leave the house to go to school, and then I had to come right back home.

SUE

Wasn't that terrible for you?

LIZ

No, not at all. I had a rope ladder under my bed, and at night when my parents went to sleep, I got out the rope ladder and climbed out the window.

SUE

Really? And your parents never caught you?

LIZ

No. They sometimes wondered why I was so tired the next morning, but they never caught me.

SUE

How long did you stay out?

LIZ

Sometimes until five in the morning.

SUE

I'm impressed.

LIZ

Didn't you do any wild things?

SUE

Well, I ran away from home when I was fifteen and joined a Hippie commune for six weeks, but then I felt like I needed a shower, so I went back home.

LIZ

How exciting. You never told me that before. That is so cool.

*(For a moment both women are silent.)*

SUE

You know, when I come to think of it, our daughters are really quite boring.

LIZ

You're right, Facebook and diaries…

SUE

Dirty rooms… how boring.

LIZ

It's too bad they never do anything exciting.

SUE

Life was sure a lot more fun when we were young.

## SCENE 10        JEWELRY

*(We see a boy, Tony, standing in front of a table with a jewelry box. He is trying on jewelry. He looks toward the audience as if there were a mirror just in front of him. He puts on some earclips.)*

TONY

Ouch, that hurts a bit… But they really look cool. Kind of like a pirate.

*(He picks up a necklace.)*

TONY

I always like it when my mother wears this necklace. It makes her look so… so elegant, like a film star or something.

*(He puts it around his neck.)*

TONY

This isn't so easy, fastening it behind my neck…

*(He "looks at himself" in the "mirror". Then he shakes his head.)*

TONY

The earclips don't fit. I need something more delicate…

TONY

Like these.

*(He puts them on.)*

TONY

Wow, they look great.

*(He "looks at himself" again.)*

TONY

But something is missing… Sure, the makeup.

*(He takes out makeup.)*

TONY

First some lipstick. Bright red. Hey, that's really sexy.

*(He "looks at himself" again and puckers up his lips.)*

TONY

And now some highlights for my beautiful eyes. Oh, Tony, you have Betty Davis eyes.

*(He "looks" again.)*

TONY

And now a little rouge to make your face super sexy.

*(He puts on rouge. We hear someone enter the room. It's his father.)*

TONY'S FATHER

Excuse me, Tony, but what are you doing in your mother's room?

TONY

Uh, yeah, I was just… I mean, I just wanted to…

*(He tries to wipe off the makeup on his face.)*

TONY'S FATHER

Listen, Tony, it's four o'clock, and you have tennis practice. Take off that stuff and go to practice. We're paying lots of money for you to be a big tennis star.

TONY

Yeah sure, Dad.

*(Tony hurries away. Tony's father stands looking at the jewelry box for a moment. Then he picks up some earclips and puts them on his ears.)*

TONY'S FATHER *(looking at the "mirror")*

Hey, that looks really sexy.

## SCENE 11        DIARY

*(Seven girls – Olivia, Sarah, Kim, Helen, Debbie, Nancy and Judy – are sleeping over at Carol's house. They are looking at a diary that Carol "stole" from another girl.)*

CAROL

Look what I have, girls. A special treat: Mary Ellen's secret world.

OLIVIA

Is that Mary Ellen's diary?

CAROL

It sure is.

SARAH

I don't believe it. How did you get it?

KIM

You didn't steal it, did you?

CAROL

She gave it to me to read.

NANCY

No way. She never gave it you.

CAROL

Well, in a way she gave it to me. She left it on her desk at school, so I took it.

HELEN

It's locked. Have you looked inside yet?

CAROL

Sure. I picked the lock with my special key.

*(She holds up a screwdriver.)*

DEBBIE

What does she write?

CAROL

Lots of shocking stuff.

NANCY

Are you sure this is a good idea?

JUDY

Hey, it's no problem. It's just a diary.

OLIVIA

Well, what are we waiting for? Let's start reading it.

CAROL

Promise you won't tell Mary Ellen that I showed you her diary.

SARAH

No way. This is our secret.

*(All the girls laugh.)*

KIM

Come on, start reading it.

CAROL

Okay. "September 10th, I can't fall asleep. I keep thinking about Ken. The way he looked at me today. The way he said hello. Maybe he'll ask me to the dance on Friday after the big basketball game."

HELEN

I don't believe it. Who does she think she is? Ken will never ask her to the dance.

CAROL

The poor girl. She just doesn't know how unpopular she is.

DEBBIE

And Ken is one of the most popular boys at school.

*(Judy takes an iPad and starts typing something.)*

CAROL

Hey, what are you doing, Judy?

NANCY

I hope you aren't doing what I think you're doing. Are you online, Judy?

JUDY

Yes, why?

OLIVIA

Are you chatting on "High School Lovers Blog"?

JUDY

Maybe.

CAROL

Judy, don't do anything stupid.

*(Sarah looks over Judy's shoulder.)*

SARAH

"I love you, Ken. Please call me. I'll be waiting for you. Your lover, Mary Ellen."

KIM

You're crazy, Judy.

CAROL

Judy, you stupid idiot. You promised not to tell anybody that I read it to you.

HELEN

Don't get so excited, Carol. It's no big deal.

CAROL

Come on, Mary Ellen may be unpopular, but she's a nice girl. I don't want her to think I hate her.

DEBBIE

Don't worry. It's just a little joke.

CAROL

I don't think it's very funny at all.

NANCY

Come on, let's read some more.

JUDY

Yeah, give us some more juicy details.

OLIVIA

I don't think we should.

CAROL

Okay, just one more entry. From yesterday: "October 12th, I heard Ken talking to his friends about me. He told them I looked like a kangaroo. He said I probably lived at the zoo. Why did he say that? It makes me feel so sad. I want to kill myself."

*(Silence.)*

SARAH

Hey, that's really scary.

KIM

I don't want to hear anymore.

CAROL

I'm going to put the diary away.

HELEN

Come on, Carol, one more entry.

CAROL

No way.

*(The phone rings.)*

DEBBIE

Who could that be?

*(Carol looks at the display.)*

CAROL

It's Mary Ellen.

NANCY

Don't answer the phone.

JUDY

I'll answer it.

OLIVIA

Don't do it, Judy.

CAROL

This has gone too far, Judy. Don't answer the phone.

*(Judy answers the phone.)*

JUDY

Hi, Mary Ellen. It's me, Carol... Stop it, Ken. I'm talking to Mary Ellen on the phone. Stop kissing me, Ken. Of course, I love you, Ken.

*(Judy laughs and hangs up.)*

SARAH

I don't believe you did that, Judy. That is really mean.

KIM

What did you do that for, Judy?

CAROL

How can I ever talk to Mary Ellen again?

HELEN

Don't get so excited, Carol. Keep cool.

CAROL

How should I keep cool? What if Mary Ellen really kills herself? Like that one girl did on the Internet.

DEBBIE

It isn't your problem if Mary Ellen is an idiot.

CAROL

But she trusted me with her diary.

HELEN

No, she didn't. She left it by mistake on her desk, and you took it. You stole it.

NANCY

She'll never forgive you, Carol.

JUDY

Oh, Carol, maybe you should kill yourself, too.

SARAH

And you, Judy, shut up, or I'll tell the whole school that you're in love with Ken.

*(All the girls – except for Judy – laugh.)*

## SCENE 12        KEYS IN THE LAKE

*(A boy and a girl are standing in front of the audience – they are looking at a "lake".)*

TONY

It's a nice evening, isn't it? So warm.

BRITNEY

Yes, and the full moon is beautiful.

TONY

On nights like this I wish I could get in a car and drive until the sun comes up.

BRITNEY

That would be great. Just drive and drive and drive all night long.

TONY

And then have breakfast at a little café by the sea.

BRITNEY

You're very romantic, Tony.

*(Suddenly Tony sees something on the ground.)*

TONY

What's this?

*(He picks it up.)*

BRITNEY

It's a key.

TONY

A car key.

BRITNEY

That's terrible. Somebody lost their car key.

TONY

It's a key to a Ford Mustang.

BRITNEY

How do you know?

TONY

We had a Mustang when I was a kid.

BRITNEY

What should we do with it?

TONY

Well, the owner probably has a second key.

BRITNEY

Do you think the owner is a man or a woman?

TONY

Probably a man. Mustangs are men's cars.

BRITNEY

Maybe it's a woman who really likes cars.

TONY

But how did she lose her key?

BRITNEY

Maybe she drove her Mustang into the lake and jumped out with the key before the car sank. And then she lost the key.

TONY

In that case we should throw the key into the lake.

BRITNEY

Why?

TONY

For good luck.

BRITNEY

That's a good idea. Let me do it.

TONY

Here.

*(Tony gives her the key. She throws it in the direction of the audience.)*

BRITNEY

Now the key and the car are together at the bottom of the lake.

TONY

How sweet.

*(Suddenly a man comes running up in a jogging outfit, it's Jonny.)*

JONNY

Have you two seen a car key?

BRITNEY

What kind of car key?

JONNY

A car key for a Ford Mustang. I lost it while I was jogging.

TONY

No, we haven't seen a key.

*(Tony glances at Britney.)*

BRITNEY

What does the key look like?

JONNY

Like a key to a Mustang.

*(Tony and Britney exchange glances.)*

TONY

Oh really? A Mustang, huh?

JONNY

My girlfriend is going to kill me. It's her car, and she only has one key. If I don't find it I'm dead.

*(Britney looks at Tony.)*

BRITNEY

Got a swimming suit?

TONY

I'll take off my shoes.

*(Tony takes off his shoes and walks into the "lake". We hear a splashing sound.)*

## SCENE 13        LOCKER

*(Two girls, Karen and Susan, are standing in front of a closed locker.)*

KAREN

This is her locker, isn't it?

SUSAN

Yes, it is.

KAREN

You really want to open it?

SUSAN

I'm not sure.

KAREN

It's no problem now. I mean, she's dead, so she won't care.

SUSAN

But I feel like I'm breaking in.

KAREN

What's the combination? I'll open it.

SUSAN

I don't think this is right.

KAREN

Come on. You were her best friend.

SUSAN

I don't think she has anything bad in there.

KAREN

Who knows? She killed herself with sleeping pills. Maybe she has more pills in there. It wouldn't be good if her parents found them.

SUSAN

Okay. 15-55-23.

*(Karen opens the lock.)*

KAREN

What a mess!

SUSAN

It looks like chaos, but it was like home to her.

KAREN

Hey, what's this?

SUSAN

That's her diary.

KAREN

Cool, let's read it.

SUSAN

I don't think we should.

KAREN

Just one entry, then we'll put it back.

SUSAN

Let me read it. She was my friend: "September 10th, I can't fall asleep. I keep thinking about Ken. The way he looked at me today. The way he said hello. Maybe he'll ask me to the dance on Friday after the big basketball game."

KAREN

You mean, she really wrote that? I read it on Facebook, but I thought the other girls just made it up to bully her a bit.

SUSAN

They were so mean to her. If you ask me, they killed her by posting all that stuff about her online.

KAREN

Let me have a look.

*(Karen takes the diary.)*

KAREN

Listen to this: "October 12th, I heard Ken talking to his friends about me. He told them I looked like a kangaroo. He said I probably lived at the zoo. Why did he say that? It makes me feel so sad. I want to kill myself."

SUSAN

October 12th. She killed herself on October 13th. It was a Friday. Friday, the 13th.

*(The two girls look at each other. They hug.)*

## SCENE 14        TREASURE

*(A girl, Gwen, is waiting at the cemetery. She has a light. Otherwise the stage is dark. Three boys and two girls join her. No one says a word. They stand in a semi-circle, facing the audience.)*

GWEN

I know it's late, and I probably got you out of bed with my text message, but our meeting tonight is very important.

MICHELLE

I hope it is. I have to get up at six, and I need my beauty sleep.

JANET

You could sleep for centuries, but it wouldn't help.

CRAIG

Girls, girls. Just keep cool.

KYLE

So what's the reason you got us out of bed?

TODD

Did you find something?

GWEN

Yes, I did. A key.

MICHELLE

So what?

GWEN

It was hanging from the big oak tree where the pirate Bluebeard was killed two hundred years ago.

KYLE

What does the key look like?

TODD

Is it old?

GWEN

It's very old, and it has a skull and crossbones on it like on a pirate's flag.

MICHELLE

You think it has something to do with Bluebeard?

JANET

Maybe it's the key to a hidden treasure.

CRAIG

And when we find it we'll be rich and never have to work for the rest of our lives.

KYLE

No more school.

TODD

And no more parents. I'll move out of my parents' place at once and buy my own house.

GWEN

First we have to find out what the key will tell us.

MICHELLE

Let's sit down first.

JANET

And we'll put the light in the center.

CRAIG

This is like a séance.

KYLE

I think it is a séance.

TODD

I'm so scared!

GWEN

Shut up, Todd. Now repeat after me: I believe in the power of the magic key.

EVERYBODY

I believe in the power of the magic key.

*(Suddenly they hear a strong wind, and a wolf howls.)*

MICHELLE

What was that?

JANET

The ghost of the key.

CRAIG

Hey, if we're going to do this right, we have to be serious.

GWEN

Craig is right.

MICHELLE

What do we do now?

JANET

I read about this kind of séance once. I think we pass the key around.

GWEN

Right. And if the key wants to speak, it will talk through us.

MICHELLE

Who starts?

GWEN

I don't think it's a good idea for me to start.

JANET

Then I'll start.

GWEN

And I'll go last.

*(Gwen gives Todd the key.)*

Well, what do you feel?

*(Todd's voice has suddenly changed.)*

TODD

I am Bluebeard. Where did you put my head after the cannonball knocked it off? I am helpless without it. I can't see where I'm going. And after I lost my head, someone took the key to the treasure chest with all my gold. Who took the key to the treasure chest?

*(He passes the key to Janet. A moment of silence.)*

JANET *(screaming)*

I am Bluebeard's girlfriend.

*(She laughs.)*

I have it! I have the key! And Bluebeard is dead. I am so happy. Now I will open the treasure chest, and all of Bluebeard's gold will be mine. But where did he put it? I think he hid the gold under the big stone on the beach.

*(She passes the key to Craig. He talks at once.)*

CRAIG

I am Bluebeard's best pirate. I never liked him, and now he's dead. Bluebeard's girlfriend took the key to the treasure chest. She must know where the gold is. I will follow her and kill her when she digs up the gold, and then it will be mine.

*(Craig passes the key to Kyle.)*

KYLE

I am Bluebeard's brother. Now that Bluebeard is dead, the gold is mine. I will follow his girlfriend and steal the key.

*(Kyle passes the key to Michelle)*

MICHELLE

I am Bluebeard's sister. Bluebeard always told me that when he died, I would get all is gold. I am the only one who knows where the gold is. The others all killed each other looking for the gold in the wrong place. Now I will go to the right place. And all the gold will be mine.

*(She passes the key to Gwen.)*

GWEN

I am Bluebeard's cook. His sister once told me that she knows where he put the gold. I will follow his sister, and when she digs up the gold, I will kill her and then I will be rich.

*(Gwen stands up.)*

GWEN

Wow, that was fantastic. It seemed so real. And you know what? The whole time I had a picture in my head of what the treasure chest looks like and where it is hidden. I almost feel like there really is a treasure chest, and we can find it together. What do you say?

*(Silence. None of the others are moving.)*

GWEN

Hey, Michelle, are you sleeping? Wake up. It's all over.

*(Gwen pushes Michelle who falls over as if she were dead.)*

GWEN

Michelle, what's wrong?

*(Gwen pushes the others, and they all fall over.)*

GWEN

Oh no, they're all dead like in the story. This is terrible. What can I do? I must tell the police.

*(Gwen runs away. As soon as she is gone, the other kids get up and start laughing.)*

CRAIG

Great. She thinks we're all dead.

MICHELLE

We really fooled her.

TODD

That was fun. But we'd better go home quickly. We'll get in trouble if she comes back with the police.

KYLE

Todd is right. Let's go home.

*(Suddenly the wind becomes very loud. A wolf howls. And a pirate's voice says: "Where's my key?" The kids scream and run home.)*

## SCENE 15        PUNCTURE

*(A girl, Sarah, walks over to her bike and discovers that she has a puncture.)*

SARAH

Oh no, not another puncture! This is the third time this week.

*(She pulls a nail out of the tire.)*

SARAH

A nail! How did I get a nail in my tire? Yesterday it was a screw. And two days ago it was a piece of glass. I have the feeling that someone is trying to cause me trouble.

*(A boy, Steven, comes by.)*

STEVEN

Do you have a problem?

SARAH

Oh, it's you again. Yes, I have another puncture. It's the third one this week. And I have to get home fast. Could you fix it like you did with the other punctures?

STEVEN

Let me have a look.

*(She gives him the nail.)*

SARAH

It was a nail.

STEVEN

Then it's a big hole. You will probably have to get a new tire.

SARAH

I'll have to call my mother and tell her I can't go to the doctor's.

STEVEN

You have a doctor's appointment?

SARAH

Yes.

STEVEN

Anything serious?

SARAH

We don't know. I keep getting headaches.

STEVEN

Then it's important for you to go to the doctor's. Can't your mother pick you up in the car?

SARAH

We don't have a car.

STEVEN

Maybe I can help you.

SARAH

How?

STEVEN

I have a big bike, and I'm a good rider. I can give you a lift.

SARAH

On the back of your bike?

STEVEN

Yes.

SARAH

How romantic!

STEVEN

Yes, well, I'm just trying to help out.

SARAH

Sure, I'd love to ride on the back of your bike.

STEVEN

My bike is just over here. I'll unlock it, and we can get going.

*(They walk over to Steven's bike. He sticks his hand in his pocket, but it comes out empty.)*

STEVEN

Where's my key?

SARAH

What's wrong?

STEVEN

I can't find my key.

*(We hear someone laughing. It's Bob. He holds up a key.)*

BOB

You mean this key?

STEVEN

Hey, is that my key, Bob?

BOB

Yeah, I found it in front of your locker. You must have lost it when you took out your jacket.

STEVEN

Give it to me, Bob.

BOB

What's the magic word?

STEVEN

Please.

BOB

You have to catch me first.

STEVEN

You idiot!

*(Steven starts running after Bob. Sarah is shocked.)*

SARAH

I don't believe it. How stupid! You can never trust boys. Now I will really be late. I'd better call my mom and let her know. It took us ten weeks to get the doctor's appointment, and now I'll have to wait another ten weeks for a new appointment.

*(Suddenly Bob comes running up to Sarah.)*

BOB

Hey, Sarah. You need a lift?

SARAH

Sure, but where's Steven? He was going to give me a ride home.

BOB

Steven is still training for the marathon.

SARAH

Don't you have his key?

BOB

It's good you reminded me. I'll put it on his bike seat.

*(Bob puts Steven's key on the bike seat.)*

*BOB*

You want a ride or not? I have a car, a red Ford Mustang.

SARAH

No, thanks. I'd rather walk.

BOB

Okay. See you around.

*(Bob leaves. Sarah starts walking away, but then she sees Steven and hides. Steven arrives, but he doesn't see Sarah.)*

STEVEN

Oh no, they're gone. Bob is probably giving Sarah a ride home in his sports car.

*(He finds his key on his bike seat.)*

STEVEN

Great, there's my key. That idiot. I tried so hard to give Sarah a ride home, and now she's riding home with Bob. I punctured her tire with a screw yesterday and a piece of glass two days ago, and then I helped her by fixing the tire. She thought I was a real hero. And now I used a nail, so the hole would be so big that I couldn't fix it, and she would have to ride home on the back of my bike. What an idiot I am. Now I'll never get a chance to take her home.

*(Sarah steps up to him.)*

SARAH

Oh yes, you will, Steven, if you promise you'll never puncture my tire again.

STEVEN
I promise.
SARAH
Then take me home, chauffeur.
*(The two of them leave with Steven's bike.)*

## EPILOGUE

*(The two MCs come out on stage.)*

MC1

Hey, you know something? I think I lost the key to my locker.

MC2

The key to your locker here at school?

MC1

Yeah. With all my stuff in it.

MC2

Like what stuff?

MC1

Just normal stuff.

MC2

You mean school stuff?

MC1

Yeah.

MC2

And girly stuff?

MC1

Sure.

MC2

And sweet stuff?

MC1

Right.

MC2

Anything else?

MC1

My cell phone.

MC2

Oh, that's why.

MC1

Why what?

MC2

I was standing in front of your locker waiting for you. And since you didn't show up, I tried to call you.

MC1

Why?

MC2

To ask if I could go to your house after school, because I lost my house key again, and my mom is staying overnight at her boyfriend's place.

MC1

Yeah, sure. No problem. But why didn't you call me?

MC2

I did, but your phone is in your locker, stupid. I had no idea it was your phone.

MC1

Oh, I see. And you kept hearing it ring? Right?

MC2

Yeah.

MC1

Oh no!

MC2

What's wrong?

MC1

My house key is in my locker!

MC2

No way!

MC1

Yeah, and my parents have gone away for a week.

MC2

You mean, we can't get into your house either?

MC1

Nope, sorry.

MC2

What should we do?

MC1

I'm not sure.

MC2

There are some blankets backstage.

MC1

You want to sleep at school?

MC2

Why not? That way I won't be late as usual tomorrow morning.

MC1

Cool idea.

MC2

We could order a pizza for dinner.

MC1

Awesome. Let's do it.

MC2 *(turning to the audience)*

Goodbye, ladies and gentlemen.

MC1

Have a safe trip home.

MC2

And if you get home and realize you've lost your key…

MC1

Just come back to school. We've got a lot of extra blankets in the back.

MC2

And pizza!

MC1 & MC2

So sleep tight, and don't let the bed bugs bite.


THE END

## ABOUT THE AUTHOR

John Reed Middleton was born in Cedar Rapids, Iowa (USA). He was a teacher for 43 years at a German school in Hamburg where he taught English, Drama and Art. He has also spent over 35 years subtitling films and translating screenplays (www.middleton-group-translations.com).

During the past 30 years he has performed his own five one-act plays (DAVID, THE DEATH OF A CLOWN, CARNIVAL AT CASTLE ROCK, KILLING DADDY, LITTLE GOETHE and DAS KLEID) at small theaters in and around Hamburg.

THE PLAYLET SERIES is his latest writing project, topical collections of scenes in English for English learners from Year 1 to Year 12 (Level 1 to Level 6) who want to perform (english-playlets.com).

By purchasing the play, you automatically obtain the stage rights.